# I Can't
# SUGAR COAT It!

RAVEN HOBBS

AuthorHouse™
1663 Liberty Drive
Bloomington, IN 47403
www.authorhouse.com
Phone: 1 (800) 839-8640

Published by AuthorHouse 06/15/2018

ISBN: 978-1-5462-4709-8 (sc)
ISBN: 978-1-5462-4710-4 (e)

Print information available on the last page.

authorHOUSE®

# CONTENTS

# INTRODUCTION

There are many perspectives about life, so I will like to tell my perspective. When we are born we have no clue of who we really are. We don't know our names, parents, our purpose or do we? We are taught to think otherwise. We are taught by our parents, and others around us what we are. We are taught how to act, talk, and what truth is. We listen to others while ignoring our own voice within. We start to see through the eyes of other people's perspectives. We are strayed away from our own thoughts and opinions. How do we take something that someone tells us as truth without question? If the truth is subjective how can they be right? Why do people feel the need to judge when we decide to follow your own truth? If we were to continue to follow what people tell us as truth will we miss out on the real purpose of why God put us here? Who is God? Do people really know who God really is? Or are we following someone else's truth about God? How about we start all over? How about we wipe our minds clean away from other people's thoughts and pretend that we are newborn's to the world. Start asking yourself some questions and see what feels like your "Right Answer" to "You." This is your key to your own happy life besides of what other people will think. Live Your Own Truth! Here is Mine!

# WHAT IS THE KEY TO LIFE?

*Is it the lessons we learn?*
*Is it the things we have been told?*
*Is it more than meets the eye?*
*Is it pain within the night?*
*Is it beauty in the sunlight?*
*Is it the path of others?*
*Is it the path we create?*
*What can you tell me about life?*
*How can you say this is how life works when you are lost without sight?*
*How can you guide me to the light when you stuck within the night of your past?*
*Can someone tell me what is the key to life cause I don't want to be lost without sight*
*Is that what you call faith?*
*How can you talk about faith when I see you playing the same games?*
*No one on earth can tell me the key to life but maybe I am the key you cannot see*
*Maybe I am the light shining on your path*
*I can show you a new way based on my unknown*
*So, are you ready to take that chance?*
*Are you ready to leave your burning past?*
*Or are you going to continue to try to show me your path of pain and games?*

# ILLUSION

*The feeling you feel is not your own*
*The feeling you identify with is not who you are*
*You carry a shell which you call a body*
*You are a soul who has become awaken*
*You were lost but now you truly see*
*You are experiencing something you think is real*
*This is just a dream*
*Don't get caught in the illusion*
*Your thoughts are controlling what you feel*
*There is no right nor wrong*
*Create what you want to see*
*Become what you want to feel*
*Suffering is NOT your birthright*
*Fully believing in your thoughts is foolish*
*Open your eyes to become your greatest joy*

# Your Power!

*The power within is something we take for granted*
*The power within allows us to see beyond the picture of life*
*The power within can take us into impossible worlds*
*The power within can bend what we call reality*
*The power within is a power you can take control of*
*The power within is something magical*
*The power within is how we can change perspectives*
*The power within is your key of life*
*The power within is your calling*
*The power within is the true you*
*The power within is ready for you to become one with its love*

# HOPE!

*Sometimes negative things can come with an disguise*
*Sometimes problems come up in an bad surprise*
*Sometimes people start to look different to you*
*Sometimes life doesn't seem real to you*
*Who knew that this day will come?*
*The day that sorrow becomes known*
*The day that people can no longer sing their own song*
*We became walking ghost trying to find the right way*
*We became hopeless with no one to tell us the way*
*How did we get here?*
*How did life turn to the worst?*
*How do we get to a place to love like the beat of a drum?*
*We fall*
*We crash*
*With no one to reach for our hands*
*What can we do to find each other even though we are right here next to each other?*
*I can see you and you can see me but we can't see*
*We can't see the pain, lost, and burns on each other's skin*
*We think we are alone but we are more closer within our souls*
*Now it's time to dive deep together and open our eyes to the beauty that we hold*

## OUT OF THE DARKNESS

*Out of the darkness you can't see the light*
*Out of the darkness you become frighten without sight*
*Out of the darkness you panic for someone to save you*
*Out of the darkness you lose your faith and hope in things*
*Out of the darkness no one can tell you that you do not hurt*
*Out of the darkness you can become cold as winter storms of ice*
*Out of the darkness you become stronger without knowing your power*
*Out of the darkness is where you hold the light in your darkest hands*
*You fire up that light and finally see the dreams you been wishing for*
*You set your own self free from the night of pain*
*You were the key to your own destiny*
*The power that can change into anything you want to be*
*No judgement*
*No pain*
*No grief*
*No one to clap their hands*
*But you stand within your power to become whole as god swims through and around you*
*You are the god of the night and light*
*So, it's time to choose your fate in your right sight*

# THE LIGHT CAN BECOME SO BRIGHT

*The light can become so bright we turn away from it*
*The light can become so bright we don't even take notice of it*
*The light can become so bright we mistake it for darkness*
*The light can become so bright we start to fight for it*
*The light can become so bright we lose trust in it*
*The light can become so bright we start to cry for it*
*The light can become so bright we don't even feel it*
*The light can become so bright we start to doubt it*
*The light can become so bright we never take a chance on it*
*The light can become so bright we start to blame it*
*The light can become so bright we mistreat it*
*The light can become so bright we start to miss the lessons in it*
*The light can become so bright we forget we are it*
*If light is us then we have turned away from ourselves*
*We don't take notice within ourselves*
*We mistake ourselves*
*We fight within ourselves*
*We lose trust within ourselves*
*We cry within ourselves*
*We don't feel within ourselves*
*We doubt within ourselves*
*We never take a chance within ourselves*
*We blame ourselves*
*We mistreat ourselves*
*We miss the lessons within ourselves*
*We are creation that creates*
*We are more powerful than you think*
*We are endless possibilities*
*The light can become so bright...*

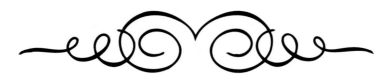

# PAIN?

*We go through the idea of what we think life is*
*We believe in the thoughts that cause us to suffer*
*We believe life is against us*
*We protect our hearts with walls to keep pain out*
*What if I told you the wall you built was to keep pain in*
*We think it's protection*
*What we really doing is hurting ourselves*
*We become trapped within an emotion which cause us to stand still within time*

*We love it*
*We carry it*
*We defend it*
*We wear it*
*We become blind to it*

*We can never See love*
*We can never Feel love*
*We can never Smell love*
*We can never Taste love*

*We are blocking out the one thing we want the most (LOVE)*
*When pain came to visit us in the past it wasn't to hurt us*
*It came to teach of something*
*It hurt so bad we thought it wasn't right to feel that way*
*Pain isn't wrong nor right it is an experience just like love*
*Pain is caused by a thought we think and the meaning we give that thought*
*Once we change the meaning of the thoughts we think that caused us pain we will began to see the beauty on the other side*
*Life is based on thoughts which gives us an emotion that causes us to react*
*Change your thoughts*
*Change your world*
*Love more*
*Hurt less*

# Don't get caught up

Don't get caught up in your thoughts
Don't get caught up in your words
Don't get caught up in your beliefs that you think is true
Don't get caught up with the things you can't explain
Don't get caught up with the feelings that are not your own
Don't get caught up in your rights and wrongs
Don't get caught up with the voices on the other end
Don't get caught up in a world that's not real
Don't get caught up in your illusion because your illusion can take you into a deeper whole
You are God in a human body
You are power within itself
You are energy that cannot be destroyed
You are more than what you give yourself credit for
Learn about yourself
Embrace the power you had all along
Wake others and see the love you cherish throughout the stormy night
Don't get caught up, just wake up

# THE POWER YOU HAVE

*The power you have is the power of focus*
*The power you have is like no other*
*The power you have can change worlds*
*The power you have has endless possibilities*
*The power you have can cause you pain*
*The power you have can make you brave*
*The power you have can make you think you are weak*
*But is it the power or what we have been condition to think*
*Are we here to play tricks or are we here to awake?*
*What are we doing?*
*Are we pushing each other to bring strength that is caused by pain*
*We see pain everyday so it's time to switch the pain to strength*
*The strength that we can no longer break*
*The power of strength that changes us to see the beauty everyday*
*The power that no one can break*
*The power that we can taste*

# Time is Now

*When will it be the right time*
*When will it be okay to say goodbye*
*When will it be just dreams manifesting in front of our eyes*
*We spend so much time in the past we can't see the present holding our hands*
*It's time to shed the feelings we once held and allow the love to take over*
*Trust yourself to become pure*
*Trust yourself to let everything go*
*Cause you are the creator to teach and to walk through burning walls*
*You are everything your thoughts hold*
*So, believe and allow your story to unfold*

# UNVEILED

# Is it Magick?

*Is it magick that I saw you*
*Is it magick how you caught my eye*
*Is it magick that you keep passing through*
*Is it magick you took the first move*
*Or is it an illusion*
*Please don't call it an illusion*
*The way you walk and the way you talk it has to be magick*
*Just keep passing through to make more magick*
*Something is telling me you are my illusion*
*I need to turn my illusion into magick*
*Beautiful, Beautiful magick*
*Are you ready?*
*Say you ready...*
*My magical illusion*

# YOU

*How can this be possible?*
*Everywhere I look you are there*
*Are you here to mess me up?*
*Or are you here to put gold in my hands?*
*How can I function with you there?*
*You are sweet as night*
*And your kisses taste like warm tea under a candlelight*
*You take my breath away when I'm near you*
*I want the seduction more and more*
*No, I was on the right track so how did you get here*
*This has to stop but when you touch I feel the mystery in our hands so take me*
*I want complain*
*How can this be possible?*
*You are becoming more than I imagine but I don't mind*
*So, continue to kiss me until it's our last goodbye*

# WHAT IS IT ABOUT?

*What is it about you when I see you?*
*Is it the look in your eyes when you see me?*
*Is it the touch you give me?*
*Is it the warm kisses that defines the passion inside of me?*
*Is it the mystery of you and me?*
*Is it the journey we are willing to seek?*
*What is it about you when I see you?*
*Should I trust the unfolding and allow the sweet taste?*
*Or should we call it quits before it's too late?*
*What is it about you I can't see through?*
*Maybe it's the pain covered over you shield of musical notes you play at night*
*Its more to you that I will like to get to know but first let's enjoy the passion under the sunlight*
*I want to see you kiss me and touch me*
*Let me be the one to show you how life is done*
*Let me pull you into the light and allow you to see beauty in a different moonlight*

# STAIRWAY

*You are always there when I turn the corner*
*You are always there watching me as I look over my shoulder*
*You are always there undressing me from a stare*
*You are always there to kiss me on the stairs*
*You are always there sitting with me so time can pass through*
*You are always there when no one can see us but us too*
*It's like magic helping us clear the way to make passion between myself and you*
*So, let's continue to make this thing a fantasy that has come true*

# You Missed Out

*We became lost without the spark*
*We were supposed to become one within our power*
*You dropped the ball so now it's too late*
*You were the player playing your ways*
*I observed as you played but now I am ahead of the game*
*You thought you had it but truth is I was the star that landed*
*I wish you well*
*I hope you become the music you always hoped for*
*I will continue to express my words as you walk by your open door*
*We will meet again but I hope you catch up to the high ends where I will*
*be standing with the palm trees moving through the wind*

# ONLY IF

*The road can be as beautiful as we make it*
*The road can be as easy as we allow it*
*The road can have plenty of unconditional love to fulfill our spirits every single day*
*The road can be over flowing with roses to keep us on the wave of kisses*
*The road can be as much as we want it*
*The road is our road holding hands together*
*The road is our tunnel vision like you said when our eyes meet daily*
*Can we hold on?*
*Can we cherish the high?*
*Can we kiss the past goodbye?*
*Can we start a new right here without thinking twice?*
*We are the souls that has mate*
*You are me and I am you so let's explore*
*Explore the beginning and the end of this kissful journey before our*
*time washes through with nothing to hold on too*

## MY BEST FRIEND

*You are my best friend and I wouldn't want to change that*
*You are a great man never lose that*
*You are more than what you see just know I see every part of you*
*I know I give you comfort*
*Just wish I could be that comfort in your own home*
*But I know changes can be scary for you*
*But just know if you jump it will be beauty you will be holding on too*

# I Wanted You

*I wanted you but you had loads I couldn't carry*
*You had beauty with touches that I couldn't erase*
*How could you become misplaced when I saw the future of happiness take its place*
*I wanted to give you all of me*
*All of me*
*I loved you without thinking twice*
*You were my all but you chose her*
*I'm not mad I'm just sad we couldn't see the beauty of you and me*
*The dream we were meant to be*

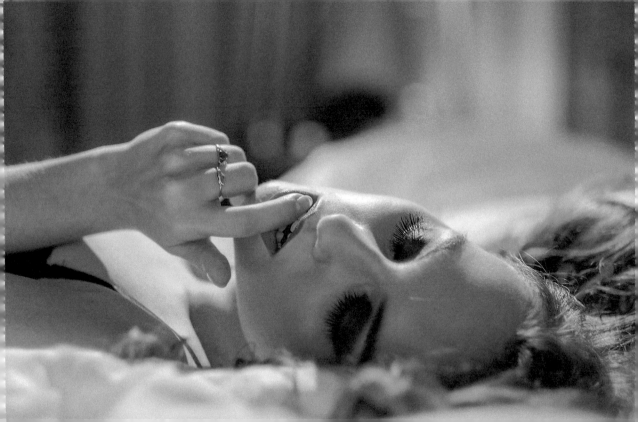

# PASSION I HAVE

*I can't have you if she's there*
*I can't have you knowing this fear is here*
*Here within me*
*The fear that I try not to think*
*The fear that has me all over the place*
*The fear I try to shake off day by day*
*But you see something different*
*The place that I will like to be in*
*The place of fearless and wisdom*
*Damn, what a good place*
*But she is there so how could I think otherwise*
*That thought never cross your mind*
*Of course, it does*
*But we want each other*
*I love you and You love me*
*But why is it so hard for our hearts to meet*
*Am I thinking too much?*
*Or maybe I am trying to avoid the pain*
*The pain that this may cost*
*Or maybe I should say Fuck it*
*This feeling has me rushing*
*Rushing to be with you*
*But I have to slow down because you are my best friend*
*I know I can love hard*
*Call me crazy but I just thought you were the one*

# Memories

*We had honesty like no other*
*We had a spark that got us addicted to one another*
*We couldn't let go even though the situation didn't look right*
*It was just you and me*
*Every night as we made it to be*
*I will never forget you*
*And the great memories we created*
*I hope I will stay in your memory more than she do*
*I wanted more and I knew you couldn't make that big move*
*But I pushed and I pushed*
*Don't hate me for trying*
*I am passionate about what I want*
*But being your best friend is enough*

# SURRENDER

# CREATE

*The power of creation is in your hands*
*Don't let no one try to take your stand*
*The power you give is the power you can bare but don't let no one take control of what you have*
*Create what you enjoy and allow the beauty to unfold*
*Nothing is in your way so don't let others pass with negative things*
*You are God wishing on a star but what if I told you*
*You are the star shinning with grace*
*Will you take that chance to be the all-powerful things or will you die hoping for change?*

# THE UNKNOWN

*The unknown world can make you become lost*
*The unknown world will have you doing things you never thought of*
*The unknown world is created by your own power of thoughts*
*The unknown world is what you believe in the most*
*This is thoughts talking to itself*
*Some thoughts are beautiful while others are crucial*
*Be the thought you want to experience and watch a whole new process of unknown beauty*

# FEAR

*Fear can withhold you from your true self*
*Fear can become the mystery of the unknown*
*Fear can become the ruler of your own mind*
*Fear is the doorway to the beauty of your world*
*The doorway to peace*
*The doorway to other things*
*Embrace what you have been withholding from and learn the true value of the power you have*
*To create realms in this mystical world of wars*

## SHINE BRIGHT

*Now is your time to shine*
*Now is your time to put your power into your craft*
*Now is the time to paint your canvas*
*Now is the time to stand tall and move past negative things*
*You got the keys to your kingdom*
*Now embrace what you have been missing*

# REALITY

*Your reality is what you focus upon*
*Your reality can make you become lost*
*Your reality is the gateway to your freedom*
*Your reality is nothing more but the collection of thoughts you been holding*
*Your reality is not reality within itself*
*It's the beliefs you have been told*
*It's the thoughts you believe are true*
*Create your own truth and began to see what reality hold for you*

# TRUST

*To be guided you have to trust*
*To be guided you have to do what's best*
*To be guided you have to put somethings in the past*
*To be guided you have to create light on your path*
*Let go and Let Spirit*
*Surrender to the love that was in you all along*
*Embrace the uncertainty of life and take charge of this beautiful world we call home*
*The power was in you all along*
*Feel it*
*Taste it*
*Make love to it*
*Be brave*
*Let it take you to a better wave*
*Trust in your guiding light that has welcome you home day by day*

# BEAUTY

*How beautiful it is to have it all*
*How beautiful it is to lose it all*
*How beautiful it is to stand your ground*
*How beautiful it is to fall down*
*How beautiful it is to love*
*How beautiful it is too*
*Hoe beautiful it is too*
*How beautiful it is too*
*Wow, how could you get lost in finding the beauty*
*Is the mind that messed up that beauty can't show up for you*
*How did we lose sight of counting the beauty and wonder of things?*
*Stop counting the ugly as ugly and start counting the ugly as beauty*
*How beautiful it is too*

# SURRENDER

*We run away from how we feel*
*We run away from life lessons*
*We run away from our fears*
*We run away from people we love*
*We run away from the present moments*
*We run away from our past*
*We run and try to prepare for the worst*
*We run away from our connections*
*We run away from helping hands*
*We run away from hope*
*We run away from trust*
*We keep running even when our bodies tell us to stop*
*We keep running towards what we think will make us happy but we are just fooling ourselves*
*You can't win if you keep running*
*It's time to surrender and allow life to run through us*
*This is bravery*
*This is love*
*This is what you been running towards*
*This is the life of the Gods*

# BALANCE

*Life has its turns but how can we catch on*
*Life has beautiful moments but why can't we see them*
*We see more of the pain but what is pain*
*The pressure we all feel not knowing the person next to us is going through the same thing*
*Where is the pain killer?*
*I was told it was laughter that keeps screaming our name*
*The part we ignore every single day*
*Why is it so hard to listen when we are reaching for it day by day?*
*Maybe it's the cloud that never goes away*
*The cloud that we can't bare to be a part of but maybe we forgot the balance of our own nature*
*The balance between sadness and laughter*
*Don't shut one out to keep one in*
*Allow both so we can become whole again*

# I AM!

*I am all that I am*
*I am everything that exist*
*I am you*
*I am one*
*I am creation*
*I am love*
*I am peace*
*I am anger*
*I am all in one*
*I am many things*
*I am earth*
*I am space*
*I am more than myself*
*I am magic*
*I am but a dream*
*I am life*
*I am nothing so I am something*
*I am what you see*
*I am many names*
*I am emotions*
*I am thoughts*
*I am words*
*I am actions*
*I am what you dream to be*
*I am spirit*
*I am human*
*I am that I am*

Printed in the United States
By Bookmasters